The Truth Within The Mirror

By
Fiona Jones

Dedication

To survivors,

you are not alone.

"I hear you, I believe you, and I see you"

Acknowledgements

I would like to express my heartfelt gratitude to the people who are close to me and believe in the importance of sharing my story. It has taken me 12 years and a memorable girls trip to gather the courage and send my story for publication. Throughout this journey, my husband has been an unwavering source of faith and support. He is my eternal partner, standing by my side as we navigate through life's wonders together.

My children hold the key to my existence, reminding me every day why I am here, why I breathe. They have shielded me from being consumed by my fears and emotions, and they are the reason why I aspired to become a mother. While I acknowledge that I am not perfect, I strive relentlessly to improve myself, both as a person and as a mother, for them and for all my cherished loved ones.

I am forever grateful to have the privilege of pursuing my dreams, and this would not have been possible without the unwavering support of truly remarkable people who have stood in my corner. To each and every one of you, thank you from the depths of my heart. Your belief in me has propelled me forward, and I am profoundly grateful for your presence in my life.

Lastly, I just wanted to acknowledge everybody on my writing team for being there and helping me through this process.

About The Author

Fiona Jones is an independent, strong-willed, and tenacious woman. She grew up in a small town in Massachusetts. She is married to her best friend and partner in crime, and together they have four children, forming a blended family. Now that all the children have grown up, Fiona is running a business alongside her husband.

Contents

Introduction

I know that I CAN'T CHANGE THE WORLD but MY WISH for you, the reader, is for you to know that you are not alone when you **STAND IN THE RAIN**. Some songs came from the people that have helped me and I give them to you so you know I am there with you. During this **AMAZING** journey, I had found **that THE CLIMB** to my destiny is where I have found who I truly am. I pray that the person who you are will learn, as I have, that the darkness can't last forever. I had made **THE PROMISE** to myself that **I WON'T LET YOU GO** and **I WON'T GIVE UP** and I hope you won't either. **The GIRL ON FIRE** is worth the fight. I believed it and within these songs the words helped with my recovery.

Brad Paisley, Rascal Flatts, Superchick, Aerosmith, Miley Cyrus, Tracy Chapman, Rascal Flatts, Jason Mraz and Alicia Keys...

-F.J.

A few years ago, I had the opportunity to meet this amazing person. This person has helped me with working through my life challenges. She doesn't know that she had such an influence in my recovery. This person had sparked something inside me. She had inspired me to break free from the prison that I had lived in. The depths of her words were as deep as the look in her eyes as she spoke to me of the darkness that has kept her up late at night. As she talked to me, I reflected on my own life. I could relate to her on some level which I had kept to myself. In her eyes, I saw her pain along with the desperation of not showing too much of herself. She has continued to maintain the mask which she has worn for years. I, myself know how it is to feel vulnerable and trying to hide what is really going on inside. Why this person had talked and shared with me as she did, I don't know. I wrote this book because I have found my voice. I have hoped that this book can help others to find their own voice. To know they are truly not alone and what has happened to them should be heard. I know after working where I do, that what has happened to me has happened more often than not. I can say that my life could have been worse. I could have made many different choices for myself.

I believe full heartedly that one person can make a difference. I can say that I am one of the lucky ones because I have had many people throughout my life who have made a difference to me. Some of them are the women that I am unable to recognize in this book. I have met many beautiful strong women.

They battle with their demons along with themselves daily. If this book does land in one of their hands and helps them to believe that they can do it, then they can beat their demons by learning from their past and to stop the cycle that they know is continuous. Their future has not happened yet. It is not predetermined. I would like to say to them, "Believe in yourself. Love yourself more than the fear that holds you down."

I know if I had given up on this quest, the quest to help myself, I wouldn't have been able to complete this book. I would still be waiting in my own dark cell wishing I could get out. I sat there seeing what I thought was weakness and in fact it was my strength being over shadowed by the fear of the unknown. I would ask myself, if I let all that is in me and all that I knew out, then what would be left of me? I needed to stop wishing to be free. I needed to not be scared of being free. How worse can my life get by doing the work that needs to be done? To face the fear because I am still the same. I was comfortable sitting here behind these bars, bonded by my past. Emotionally, this is what I had known what was safe to me (only because I have learned to live this way for so long). I still had this burning desire to know what life would be like if the walls were gone. I dared to dream, to change the course that my life was at. To dream outside of the walls that I have lived in. I feared for so long of the unknown and I learned that change begins with me. Even small changes make a difference. I am ready to break the chains of my past.

(On this day, to me, proof was shown that one person can make a difference.)

One of these women who I wish to acknowledge had said to me before parting ways "Thank you, you made a huge impact on my life and I will never forget you. I'm not going to get all emotional on you, so I will keep it short and sweet and I'll end this with a quote "To the world you may be one person, but to one person you may just be the world."

C.M. 6/11

I dared to dream.

And I found,

Me.

Chapter 1

02/16/13

Hello to me. It has been quite a while since I have written to me. I have not given myself the attention that I once did. I began running this year and as much as I say that I don't like it, I really do. When I run, I escape into my thoughts or I think of nothing at all. I would focus on my breathing and I can focus on what happen that day, that week, that month or to think about what's to come or how to handle something if it did come up. I run and play the "what if" games. I think about the kids, and how big they are getting. I think about the choices that I make for them and hope that they are the right ones for them. I have done some growing too. I make a point to play a game or read a few books to the younger children and D. J. and I are connecting better. I try to figure out my bills and where I would like to be. Wherever that may be, Brian has helped me on getting myself back on track.

Chapter 2

Today, I have decided that I am ready. I am ready to tell my story…

What I am about to say is my views as an adult looking back at the life which I have lived. Please try to stay with me as I go back to the times when my life had changed. I will also talk about things in the present and how my past had affected who I am. When I look back, I have often wondered who I would have been if things were different, but then again who doesn't do that.

I will begin with what is current in my life and then I will let you into a world as I remember. I am currently on a new medication and actually I think that it is working. I'm still not motivated like I hoped but once I do start on a mission, I am pretty much ready to go. I am not wanting to sleep as much or as tired as I use to be anymore. The anxiety, well that still comes and goes through out my day (some are better than others). I know that I am at a point that I can manage and deal with it better. It has been a while since I had a bad case of anxiety. There have been situations that I become so overwhelmed and feeling like my world is spinning out of control to where I just want to die. The thing that happens in such a situation is that, in all actuality, I'm just looking for a piece of control.

Recently, I received a phone call about doing a survey about the effects of drugs and alcohol. I even got a call back to do another survey with them so they could ask me more questions. I did agree to do this again. This survey asked about things that I might have experienced or might have witnessed in regards to abuse. I noticed that it bothered me and yet, I continued to answer the questions. The gist of this survey was they wanted to know if I drink or have done drugs during some of those situations of when I do remember the abuse that had happened to me as a child. They had asked if I drank or used drugs while having the episodes. They pretty much were asking if I used drugs or alcohol as a coping skill or as an escape to try and help me forget. I am not a drinker. I never was. I also was never big on doing drugs. Did I ever want to escape growing up? Yes, a 100 times over. I was about 13 years old when I began on medication. Being on medications did help me with the overwhelming feelings that I had been trying not to feel.

There are still days when I would love to escape and give myself the peace that my mind and soul deserve. I now find ways to help deal with those emotions and sometimes the emptiness that occupies my mind.

Looking back, I can see that when I was younger, medication helped me handle the overflowing emotions: the hate, rage, sadness, loneliness, and confusion. Those medications, at the time, helped me function amidst the turmoil of my childhood and teenage years. I now know that medication can only do so much, and the rest was up to me in how I needed to handle the madness.

When I had decided to end my life, I had pretty much said, "Fuck this world!" The medication was not enough to stop the impulse of my reckless decisions. As I lay in the ambulance on my way to the hospital, I realized that only I could have stopped it.

I just found out too late.

Chapter 3

When I left the hospital, I started to refuse all medications. I had learned how to live for almost 11 years without any meds. In the last few years, now 18 years after the time I had tried to kill myself, I have found myself back on medication. I was very reluctant about it. I did not want to go back to what I had tried to forget.

The life I had when I was told that I needed to be on medication.

The life that I had control over and what made me do what I needed to do. I battled with myself because deep down, I knew that medication can help and yet, I was scared of having my life repeat itself. I understand that as an adult, medication helped me deal with the chaos as a teenager, and now medication is helping me again to learn how to function with the calm I have found within myself. I see that with the calm I have found, it makes me uncomfortable because things are good. It's hard to understand that life does not have to be go, go, go. For so long, I have mentally lived running, unable to remember what it was like to sit, even for just a moment, with myself.

Chapter 4

I was abused at the age of 4 until I was about the age of 13. To me, life sucked, and to everyone else that was in my life, they just didn't get that. Every emotion, every thought, every memory — I had relived countless of times, but I was never heard. "Tiffany is looking for attention."

But life was not that bad; it couldn't have been much worse — they were right in one aspect. I was not kidnapped, I was not beaten, and I was not threatened. He was not a stranger to me nor a big scary man. He was my own brother. I don't think they can ever understand it. I think that everyone was wrong because it was family. A family is about comfort, security and love. All of that sense of family was gone for me at the age of 4. When I was 14, I told my therapist about this. During the years of the abuse, in my mind I tried rationalizing why it was happening and as an adult, I can see with clarity that I was just surviving or trying to coped. As an adult, I have had a hard time trying to rationalize how my family wanted me to just "move on."

After all was said and done, and the abuse stopped. It was no longer going on, but the damage of the abuse was still there. My mind and body could not just let me forget it or let me just move on. I could not act as if nothing had happened. My family did not recognize or believe that there was anything wrong with me. I had questioned if my family had really believed what I had said? I mean if they had believed me why would they ask "Are you sure that it was Billy, and not Mark?" and "Did that really happen?"

Chapter 5

I honestly did not begin to truly heal until I was an adult. Once I had turned18, I left the toxicity of my home. The constant pressure of getting over what had happen to my family because I had told them about my abuse was suffocating. My mother wanted the family back to the way it was. She made all her efforts to try. Regardless of my resistance, she continued to push. I began to hate not being heard.

The first time I had ever cut myself was when I was 15 or so. I got upset with my mother and took a pair of scissors and cut my arm. In that moment, I was getting my frustrations out and I had that control. I controlled how I was going to feel when the commotion in my life was spinning out of control. I had that. That was my security. To me that was normal because pain is normal. From that point, anytime that I was mad, sad, or feeling like I was out of control, I cut myself. The release that the pain had caused was the highest high that I have ever felt in my life. When things began to get worse in the house (I was about 17), the cutting was not fixing the chaos. I began to obsess on death because I felt that that would fix the mess that is my life.

It would silence the family from continuing to make me feel guilty and torn. Even when people made me think otherwise, I knew what a family should be. I wanted the choice of having a relationship with him and have it freely and not forced. Because of this, I became "crazy" in the eyes of my family because I was fighting against everyone. It was me against the world. All I was trying to do was survive in an environment that was killing me. That was my home. I would tell myself that if I did die, I would no longer have to fight the memories, the family, the darkness, and the madness that never seemed to end.

That was my answer.

Chapter 6

At the age of 17, I experienced my first turning point when I realized my desire to become a mother. Since then, I have not engaged in self-harm. Now, at 35 years old, I am a mother of three children. Over the past 18 years, I have encountered significant achievements as well as setbacks. These setbacks have contributed to my strength and personal growth, enabling me to find my voice.

When I turned 18, I made the decision to move out and live in Colorado, which proved to be one of the best choices I have ever made for myself. It was the first time I truly acted according to my own desires. Despite feeling scared about leaving behind the familiar, I knew that remaining would have been detrimental to my well-being. Leaving garnered disapproval from my family, who questioned how I would support myself. Their primary concern was the possibility of me becoming pregnant. I once stated that I would consider abortion if I were to become pregnant, shocking both of my parents. However, I knew this statement was not true, but it served to highlight their lack of understanding.

I eagerly anticipated August, as it marked my departure. Boarding the plane felt like a lifeline, allowing me to escape the suffocation I had felt in my previous environment.

Chapter 7

The first few months of living out there were amazing. I didn't realize how unhappy I had been until I tasted freedom. I felt liberated to experience my emotions fully and was on cloud nine. However, amidst this newfound joy, I encountered some unsettling flashbacks. I remember waking up at night, crying, convinced that my brother Billy was outside looking for me. I would cry so much about how i couldn't do this to myself. Although I had never felt scared of him before, in that moment, fear consumed me, and I yearned to escape. I believed he had followed me to Colorado to take me back home.

My boyfriend at the time, Dave, reassured me that Billy wasn't there and would never hurt me again. Despite Dave's earnest attempts to comfort me, I couldn't shake the feeling of unease. By the time I returned to Massachusetts, I had learned to assert my voice and refuse to be silenced by others.

Chapter 8

I was 19 when I became pregnant with my first child. Dave and I had a rocky relationship from the start. Looking back now, I see we were both young and unprepared to be a family with our son. Towards the end of our time together, he became abusive towards me. He would intimidate me and make me feel afraid. When I went back to school to become a preschool teacher, he would put me down and didn't want me to succeed. I worked full-time, attended school, and cared for our son David Jr. (D.J.). I was growing and fulfilling my dreams, while Dave had realized he was unhappy. He had cheated on me multiple times, and after that, I no longer trusted him not to do it again.

By the time D.J. turned one, Dave and I went our separate ways. I moved back in with my mother because I had nowhere else to go. I lived with her for two years until I was able to move out on my own with D.J. While living with my mother, I reconnected with Billy. I wanted D.J. to know who his uncle was, regardless of what had happened between Billy and me. He would get pictures of D.J. so he could see how he was growing. Dave and I both agreed that D.J. would never be left unsupervised with Billy. I also explained this boundary clearly to my family - that under no circumstances was D.J. to be left alone with Billy while in their care without me present.

Chapter 9

During the time DJ was 1 until he was 4, I pretty much did not have a boyfriend. I talked to my ex-Thomas, who, at the time, was serving time at the state prison. We had a relationship before his incarceration. He was my support. I found so much comfort in a person who was limited in what he could offer. I knew for a fact that he could not hurt me. He would encourage me to speak my mind, especially when it came to my family. He helped me see myself in a different light. He would make me feel so good about what I was doing and how I was raising David. We would talk about when he got out of prison, and we would go and play pool and have a beer. This man was the most important man in my life's journey. I was in a relationship with him when I ended up in Westwood Lodge Hospital. That was when I was 17.

The first day I was able to use the phone to call him, I begged and pleaded with him to come and get me out of there. The words he said to me that day have always stayed with me. He said, "I love you so much that I can't get you from there. I need you to get better. You had scared me, and I thought that I had almost lost you." I remember hanging up on him and telling myself that he did not love me because if he did, he would get me out of there. Those words have always stayed with me. I have carried them in my heart everywhere I have gone since then. He was honest with me that day when he refused to pick me up. In his words, I could hear the genuine love spoken behind his fear. I believed in his words and held them dear.

Chapter 10

Over the years after I left Dave, Thomas became my friend. He was there for me until I met Karl. When I met Karl, I distanced myself from Thomas. At that time in my life, I wanted to start a family — you know, the one with a house, a husband, two dogs, and a bunch of kids. Thomas couldn't offer me those things. I knew that if he were capable of giving them to me, he would have. He would have given me the world. He told me multiple times that I deserved so much more, and he witnessed how my family treated me. He was the outsider looking in. I knew that if I had continued talking to Thomas while I was with Karl, he would have urged me to leave him.

He would have told me that Karl was no good for me. I couldn't lie to Thomas; he saw right through me. He saw into my soul. I believed he knew me better than anyone else in my life. Even if Thomas had warned me about Karl, I wouldn't have listened because I wanted the picture-perfect relationship, and I believed Karl could give it to me. So I stopped talking to Thomas because I knew everything he would have said, and I didn't want to face it or hear it.

Chapter 11

July 2001.

When I started my relationship with Karl, I was 23 years old. I believed he was an amazing, well-established guy. He had his own business, a house, and dogs. He had recently been divorced and was eight years older than me. I thought he had his life together. However, early on in our relationship, there were signs that things weren't right. Around three months into our relationship, I lost my voice due to laryngitis. He was incredibly upset by how my voice sounded (even though it was beyond my control), and we ended up arguing. He couldn't stand to be around me because of it. Another sign came at the six-month mark when we had a disagreement that I can't quite recall. He asked me to remove all my belongings from his house, saying he wanted everything gone. That same day, I went to his house and packed up all my things, crying the whole time and questioning what I had done wrong. I had believed that being with an older man who seemed to have his life together would make a difference. That evening, I stayed at a friend's house. She didn't like Karl and saw through him. She had recognized the kind of man he truly was. I didn't.

Chapter 12

My friend Kelly tried to make me see that Karl wasn't a good guy, but I chose not to listen. One night, my girlfriend and I went dancing at a club, and I was in a carefree state of mind. Men bought drinks for both of us throughout the night, and we accepted. I flirted with many of them, and Kelly would tell me, "See, there are plenty of guys out there. Don't just settle for Karl." I ended up kissing a few of these guys after having a few too many drinks. At that point, I didn't care because Karl didn't seem to care either. That was my thought process.

The next day, Karl called me to ask why my things were gone from his house. I was shocked and confused. Kelly tried to tell me that this was a game he was playing, but I refused to listen because I desperately wanted to be married and have someone who would promise me a life and be there to share it with me. That night, I went to see Karl, and he apologized for telling me to leave. He asked for my forgiveness.

In that moment, I decided to tell him about my night and everything I had done. I thought that if we were starting anew, he should know. But I was mistaken. I heard things like, "How quickly I was trying to replace him" and "Did I ever have any feelings for him if I was out behaving like that?" I tried to explain that I had never been in a relationship with an older man who had his life together, and when he asked me to leave, I thought he would never want me back. Nevertheless, I continued my relationship with him.

Chapter 13

Feeling insecure in my relationship with Karl, one morning while lying in bed with him, I gathered the courage to ask, "Are you in love with me?" Karl remained silent for what felt like an eternity and then responded, "No, Tiffany, I love you, but I'm not in love with you." I replied, "Okay," and took some time to think about what I was going to say next. I could hear Thomas's voice in my head, telling me that I deserved someone who was in love with me and that I should be with someone better. Finally, I found the words and told Karl, "I can't see myself with someone who isn't in love with me, so after our outing to Canobie Lake with DJ, I will pack our things and leave again." I asked him to follow through with our plans to go to Canobie Lake Park, but I set some boundaries for our time together. I didn't want any affection from him. He agreed to this, although he did try to hold my hand and whisper in my ear. Each time, I moved away or asked him what he wanted.

The next day, I packed up DJ's and my belongings once again and left. I told myself that this was it. I didn't deserve to be treated this way. I didn't call him. After about three days, Karl reached out to me. He said that the house felt empty without me and DJ. He had done some thinking and realized that he was indeed in love with me. He asked for DJ and me to move back home with him. This time, before going back to him, I made sure to ask if he was truly sure about this because the back and forth was not only affecting me but also DJ. He assured me that this was exactly what he wanted.

Chapter 14

By the end of September, I had found out that I was pregnant. When I told Karl, he was not exactly happy about this. I heard everything imaginable from him. Karl said that I must have cheated on him, and that it was not his kid. Then he told me that I was trying to trap him. He swore that I better not be having a girl. He was not having it. He had said that I can give it to my mother, and she can raise it. Karl's parents then started to pressure him to marry me. I fought with myself many times about aborting the baby.

How can I have this child with someone who does not trust me? Regardless of how many times that I had told him, I had not cheated and that I did not trap him as he was so persistent with the negative feelings that he made himself believe that I did all of those things. I talked to my sister-in-law Marie about the choices that I was dealing with. I would tell her how he was making me feel about being pregnant. Being pregnant, I had thought was supposed to be a happy time, and I am just not. I had felt so bad. I would cry so much about how I could do this to myself again. Things did not turn out right the first time I was pregnant, and here I am again pregnant, and I am not married.

I had found myself stressing about how I was going to tell my mother. My mother was not too thrilled when I told her about my pregnancy with DJ. I still remember the things that she had said and her disappointments. Her statements were then on my birthday in 1996 "I knew it would be a matter of time you would get yourself pregnant. The way you carried on and stuff. So, what are you going to do? Are you and Dave going to get married?" I told her at the time "No I was not going to end up divorced like her and dad. Dave and I will get married when we were ready." My mother shunned me from her work when I got bigger with DJ. She did not want people at her work to know that HER daughter was pregnant and not married.

So here I am again 6 years later pregnant and not married. Karl told me that I can say that we were getting married.

Chapter 15

We had the date of 12/1/02. I found a dress, a venue and Karl was not happy. I knew it, he was not happy with me being pregnant, planning a wedding and he does not want to marry me. One night I did ask him "do you want to marry me?" and he told me "No, I don't." He continued with saying that he was being pressured and that he wanted to marry me on his terms and not on anybody else's. I respected that and my response to him was "don't marry me, I deserve someone who wants me to be his wife, who trusts my words and believes when I say that I did not cheat. I want them to walk down the aisle because they want to, not because they have to." So, it was settled, there was not going to be a wedding.

Chapter 15

I believe it was right around Christmas time that there was a change in him. He became a little softer and not so cold towards me. He began to give me affection again. I felt that he was trying to fix my heart that was broken by my thoughts that I was having the months before. The battles were unthinkable with me thinking about aborting the baby. When during those months I was also trying to convince this man that I did not cheat on him and that this baby was his. I had hoped that it was not a girl. Karl was very adamant about the sex. I was hoping that when the day came, he would not care because I knew I was having a girl. I thought that with one look of our daughter he would forget all of the bad things that he had said and that I can finally look at him without feeling like I had failed him. For him to see that I was being truthful with him. That he could trust me.

Chapter 16

On April 20, 2003 I went to the hospital during the night because I had thought that I was in labor. After 3 or so hours, the hospital sent me home. It was false labor. Karl was not too happy with me and the whole experience. So, when April 25, 2003 came around, I was 90% sure that I was in labor, but I was scared to even wake him up because I did not want to disappoint him if I was not in labor. At 12:30 in the morning I did wake him up because the contractions were at least 2 to 3 minutes apart. My mother met us at the hospital to take DJ for me and watch him while we were there.

At 02:46 in the morning Kate-Lynn Rose Bridges was born. Karl told me that it was a girl. He went over to where they were cleaning her up and was checking her fingers and toes, when he said the words "Hey there, baby girl" and Kate-Lynn turned her head at him. In that moment, everything seemed to shift for Karl - he was captivated by this beautiful baby girl who was his. He was amazed at how she seemed to recognize him. At that moment I fell in love with him again, feeling that all the past difficulties had been worth it. It felt like a fresh start, and that he would be a changed man, not because of me but because of this baby girl.

Later that day, after we were moved to my room with the baby, Karl had gone home to get changed, cleaned up and to make the grand announcement that he was a dad to a baby girl. When Karl returned to the hospital, he got down on his knee right next to my bed and proposed to me. He said he had planned to ask me at dinner that night, but Kate-Lynn's arrival had changed those plans. I accepted his proposal, believing that things would improve. There were more good days than bad, and I loved him, so I thought that would be enough.

I married Karl on 10/11/03. Only a month after being married, I witnessed his rage and darkness while driving home from a family party. This rage was not directed at me, but at another driver on the road. Both men lost control while driving with their families in the car. I had to hold onto Karl to keep him from getting out of the car after we were hit. DJ and Kate-Lynn were screaming in the backseat, and I just tried to calm Karl down. The State Trooper later told me that if it was up to him, Karl would have gone to jail for road rage. Looking back, I can see there were many signs this may not have been the right relationship for me. But I never wanted to give up, telling myself that the good moments outweighed the bad, and that nobody is perfect.

That Christmas, Karl wanted another child, so we tried to get pregnant again. I was pregnant by February with our third child. During this pregnancy, Karl's mean streaks continued. Being pregnant, I didn't feel very pretty or attractive. I felt huge, like "as big as a house" with Kenny. I remember buying a dress for Kate-Lynn's baptism that I felt good about, but on the day, Karl said it made me look like I was wearing curtains and that there was no hiding how big I was. Comments like that really hurt me, even though he would brush them off as, "just kidding." The little digs about my appearance really weighed on me.

Chapter 17

My marriage with Karl was short lived. We were separated in September of 2006. The last thing that he did for me to walk away from him was when he threw a salad in my face. No, that was not the real reason why I walked away, because I probably would've forgiven him for that. It was that specific day but it was what he did afterwards he threw the salad that made me walk out. When I was trying to leave with the children (DJ who was 9, Kat 3, and Kenny almost 2), he was yelling at me, asking "Where I was going? Was I going to see Uncle Billy? You know, your brother who you use to like to fuck? Remember? Was your brother a better fuck than I was? Kids you know your Uncle Billy use to fuck your mother and your mother liked being fucked by him?!"

Chapter 18

Those words, those exact words, and with the look in his eyes is the reason why I had left Karl. I could not believe that I had loved a man that would hurt me so much. He emotionally beat me down and I let him. After I had put the kids into the car, I walked back into the house and said to him, "you are a very mean man." My world crashed. I realized that it did not matter what I had done, he was never going to change. I know that I was a good wife. I tried my best. Knowing this did not stop me from feeling like I had failed.

After I was with Dave, I had independence, I was a strong individual. But over the last 5 years, I had allowed myself to be stripped down to nothing. I would look in the mirror and want to cut, scream, cry, and lie down and die. I wished so many nights that I would not wake up. We are our own biggest critics in this world. I felt completely dead inside. I woke every day and was a mother, the housekeeper, the preschool teacher - this strong person to the children. But to myself, I was a liar. I did not believe in anything that I was doing during that time. I did not care. I pretended in the presence of the children and everyone else around me that I was fine, that I had it all together. The reality is, this world just sucked again and I let it.

Chapter 19

I went back to what I had known was safe and comfortable to me - a familiar place. I wrote to Thomas. I wasn't sure if I would even get a reply back from him. I had walked away without any explanation, except that he already knew I had left him for a guy who could give me what he couldn't. Here I was, hoping that Thomas would be the one to help me find myself again. He is the only one I know who can truly see me. This man could sense my thoughts and know what I needed before I did. I knew that I needed him. When I did receive his letter, I couldn't believe he had answered me.

My family did their best to support me through the divorce with Karl. But my mother was always so dramatic. She would get in my head and contradict my inner being. She constantly found ways to instill fear in me, convincing me that I couldn't rise above this, and that she was the one who had to help me. Again, my own voice would be silenced - first by Karl, and now by her.

But Thomas wrote back to me. I went to see him. The first time I had seen him in over 5 years, it was like I was coming home as I hugged him. I could feel his strength wrapping around me. The feeling was like walking in from the freezing cold and being warmed by the fire in the room, from the outside in. Thomas allowed me to feel, to breathe. He was the inner voice that would encourage me to speak up.

I used to beat myself up about all the choices I had made, and he let me do that. But when I was done, he'd ask "You done?" Thomas believed in my abilities and trusted who I was. I needed to see that. He did his best to support me in my court battles with Karl. Thomas had no choice but to trust what I was doing, as I stood against Karl in the courtroom. He would give me a piece of his shirt to hold, and push me along, saying "I love you, Tiffany. You can do this. Tiffany, you are an amazing mother. You are so strong. Allow yourself to be who I know you are." As I said earlier, Thomas was the most important man in my life's journey. And then I left him again, after he had helped me find my wings.

I flew away, never looking back.

Chapter 20

This would be my greatest regret in life. There is this man who had given me the reassurance that I had so desperately needed. He gave so much of himself to me, and I had made him believe that I was not going anywhere, and then I did. I have no justifications for what I did. I try to tell myself that he helped me see that I deserve the world, and that was what I was going after when I had left. But I hurt him again, and I can never take it back or change it. The damage is done and the hurt is too deep.

If I could say anything to him right now, it would be "Thank you, and I am so sorry." Yet even those words would not be enough to convey how much he helped me see who I truly was, at the expense of his own feelings and emotions. He gave me so much, and I repaid him by leaving again. That is my deepest regret.

Chapter 21

This next phase of my life has been one of the most challenging and transformative experiences that has helped define who I am. I have always wondered who I would have been if I was never abused, and that will remain a mystery. However, even with the negative thoughts, I still find the strength to rise above the shadows of my past.

Over the last 6 years, I have had a lot of healthy learning experiences that have helped me find myself. I can say this now because I have reached a point where Thomas helped me believe that I am worthy of being loved while Brian showed me how to accept that love. In this next chapter of my life, I get to share more about how I have changed from the victim role I had inhabited for many years. It was exhausting work to get myself out of that mindset and become the person I knew I was meant to be - the person I am today.

This transition has not been easy, but I am proud of the progress I have made. Thomas' belief in me gave me the confidence to shed the victim role and embrace my true self. I'm excited to continue on this journey of self-discovery and growth, leaving the shadows of the past behind.

Chapter 22

Brian.

In June of 2007, I was preparing to move back to my mother's house, which I knew was going to be a chaotic situation for me. I had three kids and was in the midst of a divorce from my soon-to-be ex-husband. At the time, I really had no interest in dating or meeting new men.

My best friend Renee worked with a guy that she had been wanting to set me up with. Being the persistent friend that she is, Renee refused to take no for an answer. She told this man about my situation - the baggage of three kids and a crazy ex-husband.

To my surprise, this man, for reasons I still don't fully understand, decided to call me. I had previously refused to take his phone number from Renee, telling her that if he was interested, he could call me himself. Apparently, he took that as a challenge and reached out, despite my initial hesitation.

Chapter 23

On June 8, 2007, I received a phone call from a man named Brian. We had been speaking with each other every day after Renee provided him with my contact information. On June 12th, Brian wanted to meet me in person. I walked down the street with my kids, Kenny and Kat, to the park so I could meet him.

When I first saw Brian, he looked a lot like DJ's father, my ex-boyfriend, as he had blonde hair and blue eyes. Brian asked if we could go out for dinner sometime, and mentioned that he knew a good seafood place. Our first date was set for June 15th. I was nervous about going on this blind date with a man I had only been talking to for about a week, but I decided to give it a chance.

That first date ended up being the start of something new for both Brian and myself. From the moment I met him, he made me feel special, beautiful, and alive - emotions I hadn't felt in a long time. When we danced on his boat, his touch on the small of my back sent shivers through me. In that moment, I wasn't the divorced mother of three, I was just a woman who felt full of life again. I let my guard down and got lost in his embrace.

The date felt like a dream, and I didn't want it to end. Brian's gentle, attentive touches and the way he moved with me made me feel understood and accepted, flaws and all. For the first time in a long while, I didn't feel I had to wear a mask. I was truly myself.

When our date ended the next day and Brian headed to the beach for vacation, I resigned myself to the idea that this magical moment would never happen again. But I was grateful to have had that experience of truly feeling alive and cherished. If Brian never called me again, at least I had that memory of being so intimately seen and loved, even if just for a night.

However, to my surprise and delight, Brian did call again. My time with him opened my eyes to the possibility of finding love and acceptance again. He helped me see that I was worthy of that, something my ex-boyfriend Thomas had struggle with making me believe it. With Brian, I had a glimpse of what it could feel like to have someone make me feel as important to them as they were to me. That first date with Brian was a pivotal moment that changed me.

Chapter 24

I have been with this man, Brian, for almost 6 years since our first date on June 15, 2007. In the beginning, I was really guarded with my emotions and feelings. I had shared the details of my very nasty divorce and other aspects of my past with him. He, in turn, had opened up about his own past relationships, including his ex-wife, and how he had previously planned to retire in 2 years and move to Florida.

We had both been hurt in the past, and we were both trying to move on. Despite my initial reservations, our relationship continued to grow over the next several years. I enjoyed his company, and he would challenge me to step out of my comfort zone and try new things. To me, this relationship was never going to be anything too serious. After all, he had already made plans to leave Massachusetts before we even met.

That's what I kept telling myself, because I didn't want to get hurt again. I would just wait and see when that "other shoe would drop." I would say to myself, "Just watch, it will." I was still trying to work through the issues I had with the happiness I had found with Brian. I questioned whether this happiness was even real or sustainable. I was unsure if I felt truly comfortable allowing myself to fully experience these positive emotions, given all that I had been through in the past.

It was difficult for me to open up and allow myself to fully experience these positive emotions, after all I had been through. I had built up so many walls to protect myself.

Chapter 24

Just so you know, I'm the type of person who has a hard time asking for help. I prefer to do things on my own and avoid inconveniencing others or experiencing disappointment if my expectations are too high. If things don't work out, I'd rather take the blame myself. The truth is, I hate asking for help.

Shortly after we started dating, I had surgery, and he asked me who would help me during my recovery. I told him that the children would be with their dad and that I would be staying at my mom's place. He suggested that I stay with him and let him take care of me. It was incredibly difficult for me to say yes and allow someone to take care of my needs. I've always been the one taking care of everyone else and putting them first. I had built up a hard shell and was determined not to let him in.

On the day of the surgery, he was by my side. He said he would be there when I woke up, and deep down, I didn't really believe he would be there literally. But when I opened my eyes, he was right there, watching over me. He asked how I was feeling, and I could genuinely hear the care and concern in his voice. This scared me once again. Was he going to hurt me?

Chapter 25

Over the years, I discovered that Brian and I made everything special. Whenever we experienced something new together, we made a big deal out of it. Brian truly appreciated everything I did and always made sure to let me know that I made a difference in his life. With the help of my amazing and trustworthy therapist, Kristen, we worked on improving our communication and learning to express ourselves in a healthy way. I used to hold onto things that upset me and wouldn't tell him, often shutting down, acting out, or staying angry.

But I had to learn to open up and realize that I didn't need to walk on eggshells with him. I didn't know how to ask for or express my needs to him. Brian would tell me, "Use your words, Tiffany. They're just words." Eventually, I started using my words when I felt comfortable, knowing that I wouldn't be talked down to or made to feel wrong for asking for my needs to be met.

Brian and I complement and balance each other out. I tend to be impulsive with decisions and deal with whatever consequences arise, whether they're good or bad. Brian, on the other hand, is patient with his choices and often pulls me back from the edge when I'm prone to taking risks. He knows what he wants.

Three years ago, he was planning to retire and move to Florida. Falling in love with me wasn't part of his plan. Brian is usually a quiet, reserved person, but on October 16, 2012, during a cruise with his daughter, son-in-law, sister, and brother-in-law, he stepped out of his comfort zone. To my surprise, he got up on center stage and declared to everyone in the theater that he wanted me to be his wife. He asked if I would spend the rest of my life with him. I have never felt such immense love from anyone before. He embodies everything that is good.

Chapter 26

I am grateful for the presence of Brian and Thomas in my life. They have played a crucial role in helping me reclaim my life and realize that I deserve happiness. Their support has allowed me to pursue my dreams and even discover new ones that I hadn't previously imagined. I consider myself truly blessed. Life often takes unexpected turns, diverging from the path we had envisioned, but in my case, it has turned out to be even better than my wildest dreams.

I have found strength within myself to overcome the demons of my past. I recognized the importance of learning how to navigate life with the wounds of my damaged and hurt inner child and teenager. I took the time to explain to that younger version of myself that what happened to her was not her fault. She simply did what she was asked to do and became trapped in the fear of what would happen to her family if anyone found out. I also allowed the teenager within me to express the emotions that were buried behind my rage. I allowed myself to feel everything that had been locked away for so many years. I cried—for her and for myself.

Through this process, both she and I discovered that releasing those pent-up feelings didn't leave me empty or make me disappear. I had long believed that those emotions defined who I was, and I feared that once the work was done, I would be left with nothing. I struggled with myself, debating whether to continue the journey and complete the necessary work. But deep down, I knew that I wanted to become a person who is strong and confident, someone who aspires above all to be authentic, rather than striving for an elusive idea of "normalcy."

As I reflect on the story of my life, I realize that I have had numerous choices along the way that have shaped who I am today. And in making those choices, I have come to understand that I am strong, I POSSESS CONFIDENCE, AND I ACKNOWLEDGE THAT LIFE ITSELF IS FULL OF UNIQUE EXPERIENCES, DEFYING ANY NOTION OF "NORMALCY."

Chapter 27

The choices we make inevitably have an impact on others, much like a pebble causing ripples in still water that reach the shores. In my journey, this next part is what I have been tirelessly working towards. I have made some difficult decisions that will not only affect my own life but also the lives of others. I want to emphasize that I did not take these actions lightly; I have gained a profound respect for any victim who fights for their own justice and healing. Despite the support I have, there is still a sense of loneliness in facing what lies ahead.

In the past few months since I started documenting the story of my life, I have expanded my horizons and embarked on new experiences. During this time, I made a personal decision, without consulting Kristen or Brian, to reach out to the District Attorney's Office. I believe that this step is crucial for my own recovery. I have chosen to do what should have been done for the little girl and teenager that I once was. On May 8, I gathered the courage to walk into the District Attorney's Office alone and share my story, including all the details, with a complete stranger. This marks the beginning of the next chapter in my life.

Chapter 28

05/11/13

I sat so quietly

I waited to begin

Please state your name

Why is it

That you are here?

I began to talk

The voice that spoke

It was mine

I told for the first time

Of all the things

That had been taken up space

In my mind

Memories of the nightmares

I had lived with for so long.

Recaps of the details

That I have nicely buried deep inside

As I continued to speak

I could feel myself starting to let go

My grip on that life

Began to unravel

I started to breathe

This person that I was

Started to cry

I sat with her

She listened

I told

I remembered

I've seen

The past of the child

That I was

The memories she had feared

The ones she wanted to forget

They were all there

Just as I, had remembered.

Buried in the confusion

To why this had happen (to me)

This person wanted to know more

She asked questions that hurt to answer

I knew that they need to be heard.

Those answers,

Upsetting

For I began to feel those memories

I saw all that was done

As the words left my mouth

His smell, his touch, and his voice

Flooded my body and mind

I felt as if I was a kid again

Only this time

I told...

And only this time

I am heard.

My words

Are what makes me strong

I challenged myself

I was not allowing

Myself to break

For

What he had done

To me

I sat

Waiting for anymore questions

I had anger, hate, and rage

I felt alone, dirty, ashamed and embarrassed

I looked around the room and felt so small

I was drowning in the tears that did not fall.

At the end

I was told

You did good,

That must have been hard

And thank you

When I left

I walked out with the feelings of

Self pride, confidence, all so powerful

Happy and sad

Rollercoaster of emotions

Because this day

This very day

May 08

I took control

I took back my life

My life that I created to be

Because of me

Not because of my past

But from my inner strength, and

My tenacious spirit

That would not give up

Today the only thing that broke

Was my silence

I am proud

I told.

After that day, my emotions were in flux. I anxiously waited for the police to commence the investigation and begin questioning my parents about the abuse. I spent time contemplating how I would respond to the questions my parents would inevitably ask me. During my interactions with the team assigned to my case, I sought clarification by asking them questions. I also expressed my belief that, looking back on my upbringing, my parents did what they thought was right for our family at that time.

However, in the following two weeks, whenever my phone rang and it was one of them, I couldn't help but cringe. Self-doubt started to creep in, and I began questioning my own strength, knowing the pressure I would face from my family. To them, this chapter of our lives was over and done with more than 20 years ago. In order to gain clarity and find solace in my thoughts, I turned to writing once again. Through this process, I rediscovered my conviction and became clear about my position and what I wanted to do.

This too shall pass

> *The fear sits in*
>
> *It is about to begin*
>
> *Am I ready for this?*
>
> *Am I strong enough,*
>
> *To stand up,*
>
> *Against him?*
>
> *To justify to the family*

The position
That I choose to be in.

I'm Afraid
That I have
To defend my actions
To explain
That I am not the one to blame

I feel that I need
To make it clear,
That for years
I had believed
It was my fault.

I would ask myself
Was there something
Wrong with me?
Because
I could not let it go
Or just move on

The person I am now
Does not ask the question
"Why" Anymore
I have found MY answer

It took me years
But I finally have it

I am making him responsible
I am telling him
And making it known
That what he did to me was
Wrong.

The pebble that was thrown
The one the left my hand
Finally landed
I am struggling
In it's wake

This is not easy.

I'm
Questioning my strength
And this is what I know
The pain, the fear, the hurt
Are all real
Feeling that it will never let up
I sit with my doubt.
I close my eyes
I say to myself

My answer

For when you ask

What I am doing?

I can say with conviction

The person I am today.

I am a survivor

And this too

I will survive.

- Tiffany Jones

5/21/13

Chapter 29

The date July 15 was the day I had set for when the investigation was going to give me something. Waiting for that day, and also for the conversations when my parents learned about what I had done, was nerve-wracking. The pressure of it would make me sick if I thought about it too much. This is so hard, and I can understand why so many people stay silent. My fear was that my heart would break if my family made up excuses to justify why I should not follow through with this. I feared they would try to protect the wrong child/person again.

My mom was the first one who got the call. That day, she and I had gone out for lunch. She ran to the store and was coming over later to take Kat out shopping for her birthday. When my mother came into my house, she said to me, "I got a phone call today when I was at the store. It was the Chelmsford police calling. Do you know why they would be calling me?"

And so it begins.

"Well, mom, did you talk to them and ask what they had wanted?" was my reply to her, while I was reminding myself to breathe. I clasped my hands together to ground myself, because I knew that what I was going to say to her, she was not going to be ready to hear or understand.

My mother replied to my question, "Well, they said to me about wanting to speak to me about sexual abuse between you and Billy. What are you doing, Tiffany? What is it that you want to accomplish with this? What is it that you want?" As I held onto my hands as tightly as I could, so that when I spoke, I could do so without the raging angry teenager responding to her, I had spoken clearly, choosing my words carefully, "Well, Mom, I am going to try and hold Billy responsible for what he did to me."

Remember, I warned you that she will not want to hear what I have to say.

Her answer was, "I thought that you had moved on from this, why are you bringing this up now? Why? I don't understand, it has been years. What brought this on for you to do this? What is it that you want?"

I kept my voice even and calm when I replied to her. "If I could plaster it in the newspaper and tell the world that Billy had molested me from age 4 until I was a teenager, I would. Again, mom, all I am trying to do is hold Billy accountable for his actions. What he did to me was wrong, and how it was handled was wrong."

"It was years ago. What would it do or change to have it in the papers? Tell me how it should've been handled? How was it wrong?" her statement was full of confusion. The look in my mother's eyes was a look of a mother who had failed. I saw the pain in them, but I refused to allow myself to feel sorry for her, and I continued to fight for the child, the teenager, and show her that they had found their voice and were going to be heard.

"First of all, it would show that it was true, and all the non-believers can't deny it anymore. Mom, can you answer me this - was there ever a police report made on my behalf or was DSS notified of what I said? Mom, I don't remember ever being questioned by anyone, and that is what should have happened. The therapist, Dawn Smith, sucked. She sucked as a therapist, and I am now doing what someone should have done for me when I finally told what was happening."

She appeared shocked and asked me, "Who didn't believe you? We did what we were told to do, and Billy moved out of the house."

I answered her fiercely with the words that for so long I had held in. "YOU, Mom. YOU did not believe me? You asked me after I told you what was happening if it was Mark, not Billy. Even now, I doubt that you believe me. When Mable was getting married again, and you found out that I stepped down from being a bridesmaid because Billy was also in the wedding, you told me to put my feelings aside for her wedding and to stop being selfish because it was HER day."

"I don't understand, you had no problem being around him when grandma was dying - you were at the funeral with him," she stated with confusion again in her voice.

I spit back my words at her, "Billy has taken so much from me, and I had every right to be with my grandma when she was dying. Every right! And if you had paid any attention, mom, I did not acknowledge him."

"I thought that this was behind you, you said that he already apologized for what had happened," she continued.

Frustrated with how this was going, I felt like I was running in circles. "He did, mom, and then he took it back. He denied everything again. I see him for who he is, and he has not changed from when he was 19. I choose to be around good people, and he is not one of them, and I will continue to not have a relationship with him because I don't want to be around that kind of person."

My mother's and my conversation had ended because the children had come home. She left me with a quote that I have said before, "Well, it is what it is."

I try to understand the reasons, and all I can find is hurt. Since then, my mom and I have not spoken of that day - it is as if nothing has happened. She must think that she was right, that it will not change anything, but she was wrong. That conversation has changed me.

When my mother left with the kids, I went to my safe place that I have built for myself for this kind of moment, and I broke down in tears. I was very angry. I felt defeated that I got nowhere with her. What I took out of the conversation was her trying to protect him once again.

Chapter 30

I will get back to this part again I just want you to see the full circle of the conversation with my father so you can understand what all happens next.

I spoke with my mother, and almost two weeks went by and I had not heard from my father. I had seen him in passing when I would be heading off to work, and I could feel the tension - it was very uncomfortable. I just waited for him to say something to me.

The day he called; he asked if I had time to talk. I said that I did. The conversation starts like this:

"I received a phone call from your mother in regards to the police calling her. Can you tell me what this is all about? And if I will be getting a call from the police too?" he asked.

The teenager in me replied, "Well, if you spoke to mom already, then you must know why they had called her, and I will tell you the same thing that I told mom when she was here asking me what I was doing. Dad, I am holding Billy accountable for what he did to me."

"What do you mean? Hold him accountable? This is something that was taken care of some 20 years ago?" He argued.

I listened for the first 10 minutes to my father before I asked, "Did you only call me to try and talk me out of what I had already started?"

One of the many questions my father had asked me was, "If your brother goes to jail, how are you going to sleep at night with this on your conscience?" He also threw at me, "Well, did you tell the police about what had occurred with yourself and Mable?"

I responded with fire in my words, "Yes, Dad, I told the police everything. I told them exactly what happened with Billy and also what had happened with Mable. I did not hold back anything because I own what I have done. I have not changed anything from what I had said that had happened to me.

Billy, on the other hand, Dad, what is it that he is saying happened between him and I? Was it only massages, rubbing backs? Is that it, Dad? And I'm sure he has a lawyer too, right? So, Dad, did he admit to you that he raped me? That he made me do so many things that I should have never have known. Well, the police asked, and they got the details, and I didn't hold back. All that was done to me, I never told you, because a father should not know what his girl went through by the hands of his own son."

As I spoke, my words were clear, they were precise and to the point. I held back the rage enough that he knew that what I was saying was huge. He stated that he had never knew what did happen between Billy and I, and that he apologized for getting me upset with this phone call.

As heated as I was at the time of hearing his apology, my next sentence was spoken with no warmth from my heart. The reply I gave back was as sharp as the blades I used to cut across my wrists. As the blades were cold and numb, my tone reflected the feelings that were inside.

"Dad, I am by far not upset, I knew this call was going to happen, I was just waiting for it." I spoke without skipping a beat, and it felt good to say these things out loud. That ball that I started in the A.D.A. office was still going to roll. I will not have it stop until it can go no further.

Chapter 31

July 15, 2013 was the original date for when I was meeting with the team that had been working on my case. The week prior, I did receive a phone call to cancel that appointment. They had said that they needed more time to go through the files and get some more information. They had asked if we could reschedule, and what days worked best for me. The date was now to be on July 31, 2013, and I was disappointed with the wait. I had worked very hard on emotionally preparing for July 15th, and now I had to wait. I hate waiting.

The day approached, and Brian was coming with me to support and hear what the findings were and what was going to happen next.

Chapter 32

Today was the day, July 31st, and you know what, when I woke that morning I did not want to go to that office. I was scared again. My thoughts of the unknown and what was going to happen were making me drag my feet, and yet I made it there early. It was hard sitting and waiting. I tried to prepare myself for anything that might happen in there. I had asked myself, "What if there is no proof of what had happened and it is my word against his? What if they can't go any further than this? What is it truly that I want to happen?" All of the questions did not scare me. It was the answers that terrified me.

"Tiffany, so are you ready? Come on in."

In one deep breath, I took my first step towards the room to hear what the outcome was. Brian had reminded me as we walked together, "No matter what happens in that room today, you made it happen. You did everything that you can to hold him accountable, and I am proud of what you have done."

My mind was racing, and I was doing everything not to shut down so I could hear and understand what they needed to say to me. I continued to remind myself to breathe and to do it slowly. We did our greetings, then it began.

So, what we did find out is that your records from your second therapist have already been destroyed. We did receive from your first therapist another release form that they want you to fill out before they hand your records over. Billy did lawyer up, and through his attorney, he stated that he will never speak to the detectives - and we knew that he was going to do that, so no surprise there. We also did meet with your parents. Tiffany, do you have any questions?"

I inhaled, exhaled, and I uncrossed my arms so I could appear as if I was not scared for the questions I was about to ask and for the answers I was not sure I was ready to hear. "How was questioning my parents? Was there ever a police report made on my behalf when I was younger or any report with DSS?

The answers about them questioning my parents, I knew that was not the real thing I wanted to know. I figured that they would have been defensive because they believed they did what was right and did what they were told to do by my counselor. What I had really wanted to know was if there was a report made with anyone on my behalf. To me, that was so important - I needed to know if someone had fought for me and, by showing that he did do what I have said that he did, provided some other kind of proof besides what was in my head, or what I had just done 21 years later.

The answer was no.

I sat silently for a moment, not sure if I was hearing correctly, because if this happened now, regardless that the threat was no longer in the house, there would have been reports made. I felt this wave of emotions from rage, to sadness, to emptiness, to feeling utterly alone. These feelings crashing inside, I now hear that for all of the years that I had felt that what had happened to me was swept under the rug, was true. The detectives had said that during the time that I had disclosed to the counselor, and how the adults had handled the situation was sufficient, and that no reports were needed.

So as much as I was validated on my feelings and what had happened to me as a child, it did not make me feel any better - I had actually felt worse, because what I had always had felt was true. That was very tough to swallow (and still is). The team had to have seen my hurt on my face because all of them tried to reassure me that even though there was no report back then, they had believed what had happened to me.

As much as I wanted to know more, there was nothing else for them to tell me, and I shut down. I went into myself to process the information. When the feelings were raw, I wanted to cut and ignore the hurt and the pain that was in me. It was the reality to my nightmare that I had always thought couldn't be true. How could nobody care enough to protect me when I was unable to do so? What kind of therapist was this woman?

She did jack shit for me. I have done more for myself than what she had done for me in the years that I was under her care. She fucking sucked. My parents were just being naive and putting blinders on because it was all said and done. He is no longer in the house; I was no longer being harmed, and we can begin being a family again.

Chapter 33

I am now waiting for the A.D.A. to set up another meeting to go over what they have found from my hospital records that they could not obtain before the first meeting. It has been over a month, and I have come to terms with what I had heard.

When I had left the first meeting, the team had told me that I should be proud of myself because I am doing what should have been done for me back then. I am doing it now. Now there is a report about what had happened to me. If anything ever comes up in regards to him doing this to anyone else, we have it documented.

After I collected myself and reflected about what was said to me in the meeting, I was able to sit and write. I was just trying to figure out life again. Like I have said, life changes with me, and I can make those changes.

I sit with myself

To only find that....

For so long I have felt lost

Questioning the reasons to why I am here

Scared of knowing what happiness is

Unsure if that is what I am suppose to be

Happy

I remember how uncomfortable I was

Sitting with self

How I would do everything to avoid

Just that

I would escape, I would run,

Do what ever I could

When it became hard

Slowly coming undone

All

Because I couldn't

Speak of what I have tried to forget

Or erase what I have known

There were no words

As I sat in silence

Seeing the emptiness and feeling the coldness

I also saw

A fire that was smoldering

Covered from the ashes

My strength

Was the match that

Ignited the words

From the flick of the flames

It took sitting with me

To see what's hidden beneath

The blaze

It was rage

Unsettled from the years

I tried to snuff it out

To forget what you did.

It took courage

For me, to allowing myself to see

The girl that I was

And

No longer am I lost

I can no longer hold it in

Or put it aside

Or to just pretend nothing happened.

I can no longer ignore it

My mind, my body, my soul

Speaking words

Letting it out

Finally

I am ready to listen

To me

I am ready to face and see who I am

To find me

What a relief it is

Finding my voice

Putting sound to the words

Since that day

I had spoken

Of

The pain that I had endured

And talked about the hurt

That was buried deep inside

Since then

My life has not been an

Emotional episode

With the time that has past

A calming has swept over me

I sit now

Looking at me

And I can see

That I am

This amazing, strong

Extraordinary girl

Who has a voice

With something to say.

I am woman

Hear me ROAR.

- Tiffany Jones

I have been asked by people who know what I have been doing these last couple of months what I was going to do if I am able to prosecute my own brother, if they did find enough evidence to hold him accountable. I stated that I would take this as far as I can. I did this work not just to walk away, I did this to hold him accountable, and that is what I am going to do. As a mother now, I can see how my parents had handled the situation, and I know that I would not have handled it the same way as they did. I can say that I have not handled it the same way. I have had two incidents occur in my household where my youngest had come to me to tell me that someone had told him to do something that he knew was not okay. I, as a mother, did what I was supposed to do. I notified all of the right people. I followed up and stayed on it, and most importantly, I believed what my son had told me.

Chapter 34

Months have gone by, and I finally hear from the A.D.A. Office in regards to what is going on with the case. The woman had started off by saying that they had received the medical records from the first therapist and that they have the date that I had disclosed, which was June 10, 1992. She continued to let me know that the statute of limitations to prosecute had not expired and nor will it ever, because the law states that rape of a child will have no statute of limitations.

She also had told me that in the records they had received from the therapist, a report was in fact made on behalf of me to DCF at the time of my disclosure. She stated that it was screened out and handed over to the District Attorney's Office, and that they had felt there was no need to prosecute my brother.

While she was talking, I was doing the math with how old I was when I did tell, and how old my brother was at that time. I was 14, and I would be 15 on July 15. With that being said, that made my brother 19 at the time that I had told. He would be turning 20 that October.

I had asked, "How did DCF screen it out?" And why did we not find this record? She had said that she has already filed for the original paperwork from DCF and that she asked to get a copy of the report from the District Attorney's Office also. She had shared that she was surprised to hear that a report was made and that we had not found it before. She is also curious about the reason as to why they did not prosecute him. I asked the same thing. I said he was over the age of 18, so how could DCF screen it out? She hopes to get these questions that I have answered.

I told her that I was happy for the update, but I am frustrated about having no answers and just more and more questions.

Chapter 35

The teenager that is in me has a few things that she would like to say in regards to the meeting that I had with the A.D.A. and share her thoughts of the whole thing.

I feel like I am running into a wall and here I continue to keep doing it. I am beginning to question why am I doing this. Why am I putting myself through this bullshit, and to find out there very well might be nothing that can be done? I have been mentally preparing myself for the fight of my life. Literally, because this battle that I fight for is for ME. I am willing to lose my family to hold him accountable, and he can no longer hide behind my mother who does continue to protect him. This frustration is suffocating. I know that it shouldn't be this way, and I want to cut. I want to rip that blade right across my arm or any other part of my body.

Smash my head against the fucking wall just a few times. Scream, scream like nothing matters and that I don't care, or care who hears me, just to let this craziness, madness, this defeated feeling out of me. I can justify it, the why it was ok to cut, to why it was ok to smash my head - yeah, I can justify it because the strength that it takes to stay strong finally crumbled underneath the weight of what I feel are setbacks. Who are you or anyone to say anything different or to even judge my decision on what I do anyway? Until you have walked in my shoes and have lived what I have lived, you should keep your fucking mouths shut because you don't know what it was like or how it felt to be there. So, until then, keep your thoughts to yourself. Now this is what lies underneath the rage and anger that I hold. This is what I don't want to feel - Weakness, Disappear and Reality.

Today I don't want to be strong. Today I want to cry because I know that I can't cut or smash my head against any walls or to just give up. So I want to cry. This system sucks. I have no control on how long it will be until they find these alleged reports. My fear is that if the ball was dropped, I will be lost. I wish that the words of the Attorney mattered more. With her saying that she "believes what had happen to me," and that means nothing to me. I feel that it should, but I don't feel anything. So now I wait.... Months have gone by, and I only have time to think. I am now in December, asking myself to call them to see where they are now with the investigation. Every day that I had off that month, I would put it on my "to-do list," and every night I had gone to bed without calling. I did not want to call and for them to say that they had nothing to tell me yet and that they were still looking into the information that they would need to prosecute.

Chapter 36

January 8

I do believe that things happen for a reason. The A.D.A. has made the decision that it was time to close the case against my brother. The paperwork that was filed by DCF (DSS) in regards to my disclosure cannot be found, that DCF just so happens to have some files missing in the year of 1992. The District Attorney's Office never prosecuted my brother back then because he was currently in counseling and was removed from the house. Since then, laws have changed, and it was told to me that if this was to happen now, things would have been handled very differently.

My first thought after hearing that was "so where is my justice for what he did to me?" I had told myself that the justice for me was doing what I did. I know within myself that I have done absolutely everything that I could to hold Billy accountable. I found that with what I have done, it was for me. I now am able to have some kind of closure because I have done everything to let everyone know what had happened.

To me, my past did not define who I am, and I have with pride taken care of every part of who I am today. I broke the silence. Child abuse is unfortunately very common, and very common it is hidden. The victim hides from what is happening to them because they question how others might look at them differently. They bury themselves in the shame and the guilt.

I acted out for so many years, fighting to have control of my life, fighting to be heard. I believe that if the District Attorney's Office were to move forward, I knew I would be ready to go back to the hell that I have lived through, with the support of my loving fiancé, my most amazing therapist, and with the friends that I have allowed in.

I have grown from this experience. I learned that there are days that I made huge strides, that even when giving up was looking like the only thing to do, I continued to move forward, even if I was crawling. I am not going to ever say this process was easy. I worked very hard to be here, and I only got here because I WANTED IT. The days in my darkness, I couldn't even see myself ever finding any light. I tried to stay positive, and by God, you have the right to have days that you can break down. I cried (it took me some time to be able to do this.) It is not a weakness, it truly is a release. I screamed. I learned to laugh without having the mask. I learned to LOVE ME.

I am powerful and I am Loved,

I am powerful and I am Loving,

I am powerful and I LOVE IT.....

This was the quote I would say, even when I didn't believe it.

9 798330 284047